I0839806

# MILK TULIPS

By Heidi Lee Cross

**Thankyou …**

This book is dedicated to my partner Charlie, my son Jamie and my wonderful friends who have supported me through this journey with a special shout-out to M, you know who you are.

I also want to dedicate it to all the carers, paid and unpaid, who look after those with dementia in all its forms … my dear mum who continues her dementia journey, and my late father; you were both wonderful parents and taught me empathy, kindness and resilience.

Just a quick word about the name of the book; it comes from an incident when my dear Mum put the flowers that we'd just bought her in two *full* pints of milk. This is a classic example of how dementia can manifest, making even the simplest of everyday tasks difficult.

Milk Tulips became an affectionate term my young son and I used, sometimes you must find humour in the darkness.

Top tip: tulips don't like milk, don't try this at home! I carefully poured the milk down the plughole and rearranged the blooms in a vase, they were much happier.

I hope you enjoy reading this book.

## Introduction

If you have bought this book the chances are, you, like me, have a loved one with a dementia diagnosis. Firstly, thank you for purchasing this book, I hope it helps you to navigate the journey ahead, and if just one person can benefit from my experiences, this will have been in some way worthwhile.

Secondly, I am not a healthcare or mental health professional, but this book is intended to give some solace to those caring for a loved one with dementia, it is a personal insight and of course, everyone's experience will be different. Please seek help for yourself and your loved one during this journey (I have included a list at the end of this book of organisations, books and technology which may be of help). However, I hope my poems, personal stories and tips can help you realise you are not alone and point you in the direction of those who can help both practically, emotionally and spiritually.

Watching someone deteriorate both cognitively and physically is a long and rocky road. It can be overwhelming, sad, frustrating, scary and heartbreaking all at once.

Dementia is sometimes referred to as 'the long goodbye' and you may lose the mother, father, grandmother, grandfather, auntie, uncle, partner or friend that you thought you once knew. However, they are still there, and you will see glimmers of the 'old them'. Hang on to these moments, and even through the difficult times try to find sparks of connection, this is a hard journey for them too.

I did not feel like this at the start of my mum's decline; my father had just died, and I had a young son, four at the time. I was scared, resentful and living life in a constant state of fight or flight. Looking back, I would have done a lot of things differently. I know more now, and I can't go back in time to prevent some of the arguments, accidents and awful situations that occurred before my Mum's official diagnosis.

However, I can help you hopefully and give you the benefit of my mistakes. It may feel hard right now, but it will be ok. You are stronger than you think, and you are not alone, it's never too late to reach out to friends, relatives, and specialist dementia charities and organisations. It helps share the burden of caregiving and decision-making.

Finally, please try to look after yourself. Caregivers, especially those dealing with a loved one with dementia, can neglect their health, miss their own doctor's appointments, overeat, drink too much alcohol, or fall foul of other addictions that are ultimately unhelpful. It's a cliché but it's true, you can't pour from an empty jug and for you to help your person, you need to be well yourself, more about this later.

I hope you will enjoy reading this book of poems, tips and personal experiences inspired by my mum's Alzheimer's diagnosis and progression. Remember it's a marathon, not a sprint, so take it easy on yourself. You're doing great and remember you are not alone.

**Forget Me Not Mum**

Who am I today, Mum?
I'm waiting for the clue.
You think I'm just a friend now,
Who comes to sit with you.

You know my name and like me,
That friendship bond still strong,
But you talk about your 'husband',
Though poor Dad is long gone.

Some days your house is strange to you,
You ask to go 'back home',
Where your Mum and Dad still wait for you,
You hate to be alone.

I try to help you recognise that where you are right now,
Is full of all happy memories, I grew up in this house.
But nothing will persuade you, this history now erased,
You often wander out now, this isn't just a phase.

The slow decline is hard to watch, the good days are so rare,
But when they come, we chat and laugh, you smile without a care.
This really is the long goodbye, a journey not a sprint,
I search for those past gems of 'you', the old 'you' through the chink.

I used to get so angry … why you, why me, why this.
But with time there comes acceptance, some hope within the mist.
You're still my Mum, you took my hand, you soothed me when I cried,
And I will be your little girl until the day I die.

# Chapter 1

## Mum

"I love you," you say.

I tell you I love you too. Sometimes it's not like this, sometimes you glare and scream and shout. This is a good day.

"Shall we get up and go downstairs?" I say.

"OK," you reply.

You tell me that I'm a good girl and that you've always loved me.

"I've known you for a long time," you say. I nod in agreement. That's true.

It's been a few days since I've seen you. I feel the familiar pang. Though time is a meaningless concept to you now, the guilt is still immense, a sinister and pervasive force squeezing at my chest – joining in force with their partners in crime "Fear", "Resentment" and "Heartbreak".

You're sitting up now on the edge of the bed. I help you put your shoes on. You've never liked slippers. I pull you up to stand. We both laugh. Luckily the morning carer has already got you dressed.

You shuffle towards me. That telltale Alzheimer's gait. Your father had it too, in his later years.

"Do you need the toilet?" I say. You shake your head. I hope the carer has put you in your 'special' underwear.

I help you navigate your way downstairs; it takes effort, but you've always been determined and stubborn. You stop halfway … "There's no one downstairs is there?" you question. I say no, it's just you and me.

We get to the bottom of the stairs. "I've always liked you," you say. I smile and say, "I've always liked you too Mum".

"Where do I go?" You look at me like a worried child. Waiting to be given instructions. Eager not to do the wrong thing.

"In there," I say. I point you towards your living room. The room that's been your living room for the last 50 years. I smile with effort, that now familiar knot in my stomach.

"Look there's your mum and your dad," I say pointing towards the black and white photographs I've ensured are visible on the mantelpiece.

I help you navigate your way into your armchair. You slump down and I rearrange your pillows and put the TV on for you. I give you the newspaper I buy one for you whenever I come. You try to read it, but the layout is confusing to you now, the stories intermingle and make no sense.

I go to the kitchen and put the kettle on. While you're occupied, I check the video doorbell battery and decide it needs charging. It's also my window to your front garden – a necessity now as you sometimes decide to leave … to go 'home'. You never get far but I am always on alert … watching from afar when I can't be with you. I need to protect you now as you once protected me.

Battery now charging I have a quick look through the blue folder, hidden in the hallway cupboard. I quickly scan through the agency notes, you didn't sleep at all last night. You rarely do these days.

I enter the living room with two cups of tea, not mugs, you always despised mugs, a biscuit in each saucer. I place it down next to you. I catch you waving at someone on the television. You see me and look up. You say, "Thank you that's very kind of you". I smile.

We sit in silence for a while. You try to find the words for a conversation. "How are you?" I smile and say, "I'm ok", although I am very far from fine. I ask in return how you are. You say you're a bit achy and laugh saying, "I'm very old now!".

You're happy enough and for me, these days, that's enough. You drink your tea and say it's hot. Eat your biscuit "This is really nice!" You always had a sweet tooth. You sit for a while eating the sugary treat gleefully. This makes me happy.

You look at me again "How are you?" I reply again that I'm ok. Tell you something about my day. You look at me again "My husband is at work." I nod and smile. You often talk about your parents now too; you complain that you rarely see them these days.

We talk some more. If you can call it that. It's stunted and fragmented, I have learned to just go with the flow and drift wherever the conversation takes you. You look at me and say, "I need to go home today". My heart sinks. This is a regular conversation. You used to pack your bags and wait for someone to take you there.

I resist the urge to correct. To say "This is your home! You've lived here most of your life. I used to play in the garden and throw paper aeroplanes down those stairs!!"

Instead, I change the subject, distraction is the only way. I hear footsteps at the front door, the rattle of the key safe. Your lunchtime carer has arrived and it's my cue to go and get on with my day. Not long until the school pick up. I need to refocus.

I say hello to the carer and put my coat on. I tell you that your 'friend' is here, and I need to collect my son. You look disappointed. I say I'll see you tomorrow. I lean over and kiss your cheek … "Bye Mum, love you."

Chapter 2

## Down the Rabbit Hole

In the early stages of Mum's memory loss, there were subtle signs. So subtle, that only my father and I were noticing them. This was before my dear dad died, and he would arrive at my house and roll his eyes mouthing "She's off her head again today!"

They would have terrible disagreements; she would insist something had never happened when he knew it had. She would mention a celebrity had just died (she was into her pop culture), when in fact they had died 10 years ago or more.

One day my parents arrived to visit me and my son, Dad looked gaunt and anxious as he helped her out of the passenger seat of his car. Later when Mum was playing upstairs with my young son who adored her, he told me what had happened. It was my late sister's birthday: Shelly had died at the age of 5 after a traumatic and drawn-out decline, suffering virus encephalitis at the age of 2, which led to various complications, brain damage and extended stays in Great Ormond Street Hospital for Sick Children in London.

It was a massive trauma in my parents' life and though she'd died before I was born, I had grown up being aware of her, that and the fact that I wasn't really an 'only child', because I'd had a sister, and she was now in heaven. Every year on her birthday Mum would talk about her and get tearful and upset.

Shelly's birthday was never forgotten (not then at least) but on this day something else had happened, something which had caused undisguisable worry on Dad's face. While still upstairs he told me, in whispers, what had happened.

"Mum asked me what relationship Shelly would have had to you, had she lived."

My heart sank and I said, "That's not good, what did you say?"

He told me he'd said, "Her sister, of course, Heidi would have been her sister!"

Mum apparently got flustered and proclaimed of course she knew this. But it was a massive red flag and we both knew it.

### Sister

I never knew my sister,
She died before I lived,
I see her in my parents eyes,
The sorrow of a life not lived.

I never knew my sister,
But know that she's still loved,
And that her life came to an end,
A loss I fear to comprehend.

I never knew my sister,
Yet feel her loss anew,
I mourn today what could have been,
The aunt my son has never seen.

I never knew you sister,
I wish that you were here,
To share the up's and down's of life,
To wipe away each others tears.

I never knew you sister,
But hold you in my heart,
And hope that you have seen me,
Through a lifetime spent apart.

Chapter 3

## In Denial

Things went on like this for a few months. My dad would tell me he was concerned about Mum, they would have massive arguments, and then things would go back to 'normal' for a while.

But Dad was worried, and he mysteriously went to the GP one day, he said to get his hearing checked out. I will never know if this was the case or not, but he came home saying that the doctor had said his blood pressure was too high and he needed to keep a check on it at home.

Mum was worried, I was worried. Also, during this time, I called a dementia support line to say that we thought Mum was having some memory issues.

The lady on the phone was helpful but said ultimately, I needed to get Mum to see the GP or go and see the doctor myself and talk about my worries.

I spoke to Dad, and he said that he couldn't go behind her back. She would continue to have good days, and then suddenly fly off the handle.

Looking back, it was probably far worse than I imagined but I wasn't there, so I didn't see it, I just heard a version of it later from my dad.

Mum and I continued to worry about Dad's blood pressure, maybe me even more so because I knew a lot of it was exacerbated by the stress of what was happening with her.

I was worried about them both and navigating my son's first year at primary school. Life went on. I asked Dad if he was worried about his blood pressure and if maybe he should go back and ask for some medication. He told me it would get high and then drop down, usually in the mornings.

During this period, Mum had an issue with her ears which resulted in her getting hearing aids. A scan of the ears was involved, and Dad was pleased that nothing else had shown up on the scan of her head – but of course, they weren't looking for dementia plaques and this would not have shown up during this type of assessment anyway. He was grasping at straws.

One night I got a late-night call from my parents' home number which they rarely used. She said she'd found Dad lying on the floor of the bedroom unconscious. It was Friday the 13th 2017.

### How Do I Tell You?

I watch your deep untroubled sleep,
I stroke your hair and mutely weep,
How do I tell you when you rise?
It's grief and pain that fill my eyes.

As my chest burns with fear of loss,
You dream of rides and candy floss.
I hold my phone and text a friend,
I pray ... but know it is the end.

Sweet memories are crushing me,
Of hazy days spent by the sea,
Strong hands that lift above the waves,
Rock pools and nets and hidden caves.

Your wriggle, laugh, but do not wake,
My phone rings and I start to shake.
I see his face when you were born,
My heart rips further, shredded, torn.

He was so proud of you and I,
But time was up, he had to fly.
You're only four, how to explain,
That life will never be the same.

Your eyes flick open, you stretch and yawn,
I hold you close, it's almost dawn.
I sit, explain, watch as you cry ... last night my dad, your Grandad died.

Chapter 4

## No Time for Grief

As soon as I had that call from my mum, I knew that my world as I knew it had forever changed. My partner went immediately round to her house (I don't drive, and it was 11 pm by this point, so I stayed home with my then 4-year-old).

I called the ambulance and heard the siren in the distance, we live close by, and I knew that one was for my dear and much-loved dad. The paramedics were at the house for what seemed like hours, they managed to get his heart started but they didn't realise until later that something else had happened too. He never regained consciousness.

They spent the night at the hospital, and my partner and I were in constant correspondence by text. By morning the hospital team said they were going to switch off the life support machine. Dad had suffered a subarachnoid brain haemorrhage, followed by a cardiac arrest.

I phoned a friend who drove me and my son to the hospital so I could switch places with my partner, and he could return home with our boy. I sat with Mum, and Dad, who seemed peaceful, as if he was sleeping. They asked us to leave the room whilst they turned off the life support and took the breathing tubes from his mouth.

Mum and I sat holding hands in the family room. What seemed like an eternity later a nurse called us to come and see my dad for the last time. I won't explain how awful that image was, but it will live with me forever.

I remember thinking that he didn't have his false teeth in (he'd lost the front lower five as a teen after being involved with a hit-and-run accident, the driver was drunk) and was always very embarrassed about them and the scar around his upper lip and chin. I had never seen him without them until now – and I knew he would have hated me to have to see him like this.

We left, went to the hospital cafeteria and I got Mum a cup of tea. I called my partner and asked if he could come and pick us up from the hospital. We took Mum back to our house, but she wanted to go home that evening, so I stayed the night.

After two nights, my son was missing me badly, my mum told me I should go home, and that she would be ok. To her credit, even before Alzheimer's, I had never thought she would be able to live alone. She had married young; she and my dad had met when she was 15, married when she was 17 and him 23. She'd gone straight from living with her family to married life and had never really been independent.

I did however immediately have to sort out and take over all her finances, work out where their money was, and start ensuring everything was in her name. I was the one who organised the funeral, that spoke to lawyers, and I was the one who sorted out direct debits for bills.

During the conversation at the funeral parlour, Mum was displaying more signs of confusion. They were asking about her preferences for the funeral and about my late father. She started to talk about him being in the RAF – I gently put my hand on her arm "Mum, they mean dad, MY dad, not YOUR dad" which is whom she'd started describing.

I also began doing all her food shopping for her as Dad had done all this since his early retirement at 58. She has suffered from severe osteoarthritis for years, and so had become completely dependent on him for most things, now she only had me.

Dad had also taken her to get her hair washed and blow-dried every week as she couldn't do this herself anymore – I arranged taxis each week as I worked Fridays. When my partner was made redundant 6 months after my dad's death (yes it really was a bad year 2017), he took over the role of taking her and collecting her from the hairdressers.

Gradually our lives became smaller and smaller, revolving around her, even though her memory loss was still in the very early stages. Our lives as we knew it ended. There was however a small glimmer of hope – I found myself pregnant the day my partner found out he was being made redundant, just 6 months after Dad's death.

It was something positive, something to look forward to and I was thrilled that I would be able to give my son a sibling at the grand old age of 45. Then he wouldn't be an 'only' like me.

Things were not to be, at my 12-week scan we were told that there was something wrong. We were referred to another hospital for a CVS the following day. It turned out that the baby had Edwards Syndrome (Trisomy 18), a rare genetic condition, and was unlikely to make it to term.

We lost him shortly after this. Dementia doesn't care what else is going on in your life, and a carer's role never stops … even when you're

going through your own shit, and that is so
bloody hard.

### Angel Baby

Dear angel baby when you left, I started feeling sad, bereft,
A part of me no longer here, your life reflected in my tears.
Many didn't even know that you were in me, 12 weeks grown,
Like a secret I can't share, I think of you and blankly stare.

The words cut through me like a knife … "incompatible with life'.
Your sweet, heart stopped, with silent voice, you free me from
heartbreaking 'choice'.
The world forgets, my stomach shrinks, the hours drift by … I breathe, I
blink.
I scour the net for mums like me, who've lost their heart to Trisomy.

A world of pain we share online, it helps to talk, our words a shrine.
Life will go on without you there, your quick demise seems so unfair.
Out from the screen you waved at me, while they said 'abnormality'.
I won't forget you little one, by precious, tiny, unborn son.

Chapter 5

**Mental Health**

Statistics show that around two-thirds of dementia caregivers are women, around 34% are 65 or older, and around one quarter are, like me, part of the 'sandwich' generation: those caring for children under 18 and ageing parents simultaneously, a statistic likely to increase with many people starting a family later in life.

Caregivers often put their needs last, forget their appointments, and suffer from poor mental health, more so if they are caring for someone with a dementia diagnosis. An article published by the Alzheimer's Society (online) in 2018 stated that 9 in 10 dementia caregivers experience stress several times a week, with a further 80% finding it difficult to talk about the emotional impact caregiving has on them.

I have struggled and continue to struggle with this myself, although I am in an infinitely better position than I was a few years ago … I would like to make the journey easier for you.

Eat well; the drive to comfort eat or drink alcohol may be strong when dealing with a loved one with dementia, but fresh fruit and veg, and less processed foods will help you feel better mentally and physically.

Sometimes while making Mum a cup of tea, I have been known to inhale an entire packet of custard creams, in preparation for the continuation of some bizarre, repetitive or accusatory dialogue that we have been having. It doesn't help and my weight has increased, taking its toll on my already arthritic hip joints.

When the urge to splurge is strong take a moment and take a time out. If you're able to, go out for a walk, fresh air and nature can do amazing things for the soul.

If this is not possible, and you're a full-time caregiver, just take 5 minutes out. There are some fantastic free mindfulness exercises on the internet which will help you focus on your breathing and ground yourself in the moment. This can make a tremendous difference and help stop racing thoughts and overwhelm, though I know it can be hard to do this when the situation is stressful.

It's important to say too that the GP can help if you're feeling depressed and anxious. In the UK you can be referred, or self-refer, for free NHS therapy services if you're over 18. Cognitive therapy is good if you're after a practical way to stop anxiety, but if you need to offload, talking therapy can be more beneficial.

At a certain stage, after doing several over-the-phone talking sessions with a lovely therapist, I felt I needed additional help. I spoke to my GP and was prescribed an antidepressant for my anxiety. Whilst I know this is not the answer for everyone, this has helped me control my anxiety and given me a certain level of detachment needed to protect my mental health and put things in place for both me and my mum to move forward.

After my dad's sudden death and pregnancy loss, I was running on adrenaline. I was in fight or flight mode and started having panic attacks and severe anxiety. I pushed forward but I was burned out, my blood pressure was up and down like a yo-yo, and I was having frequent heart palpitations and chronic migraines.

Whilst medication may not be for everyone, please don't feel ashamed to take it if you think you need it, if you had a broken leg, you wouldn't attempt to walk about without crutches, and our mental health is no different. Do what you must to navigate these challenging times, and remember, this too shall pass.

Also ask siblings, family members and friends for help. I know it can be hard to reach out, but even if you can take a break for half an hour to give yourself a breather it will help you to recharge your batteries. Carer burnout is very real and very debilitating.

Please use the Dementia Support Forum too; this online community is amazing and helped me massively during Mum's early cognitive decline. You can post questions, read other stories and more than anything it helps to know that you're not alone.

These forums can also provide some helpful practical tips regarding help available, tech support and more so, please do this if you or your loved one are struggling. You can also call the Dementia UK helpline and speak to an Admiral Nurse on 0333 150 3456.

Many local councils also have carers societies, support groups and more; you may be able to get discounted access to your local swimming pool or gym, try and find out all the resources that are available in your area and utilise them. I can't stress enough how important it is to look after yourself. None of this works if you're not well and driving yourself into the ground won't help the person that you're caring for either.

Please be kind to yourself as well as others.

### A Dementia Caregiver's Wish

Forgive me, I'm distracted,
I'm trying to engage,
But my mind's still with my loved one,
I cannot turn the page.

I'm talking and I'm smiling,
But I'm worried they're in danger,
Today my mother spoke to me,
As if I were a stranger.

I'm trying to be present,
And to get out of my head,
But my stomach now is churning,
I forgot to get her meds.

Forgive me if I'm distant,
She's always on my mind,
I'm wondering if she's fretting,
And her glasses ... will she find?

Forgive me if I'm tearful,
I grieve the mum I've known,
And though she IS still with us,
Our shared memories have flown.

I need to keep your friendship,
More than you will ever know.
So please don't be upset,
If my texts are scarce or slow.

It can be somewhat lonely,
This tunnel that I'm in,
But please keep us in your hearts,
So that dementia doesn't win.

## Chapter 6

### Early Signs

So, what are the early signs of dementia? They can vary but the obvious one is memory loss. Suddenly they will start repeating conversations, forgetting things you've told them, misplacing items.

In the early stages, only the closest friends and family members might notice these anomalies, and often, people overlook the warning signs, thinking that maybe this is just the usual process of ageing.

And whilst a certain amount of memory loss is expected as we age, dementia is something different. Dementia is an umbrella term for memory loss and other cognitive impairments that are severe enough to disrupt daily life.

Under this umbrella are Alzheimer's, Vascular, Lewy Body, Frontotemporal and other causes including Huntington's disease. Often your loved one may have Mixed Dementia, meaning they have two or more of these.

Before my own experience, I thought dementia was just a matter of memory loss; but it is so much more. Not only has my mum forgotten family members, past and experiences, but how to do simple things. She often hallucinates and this symptom started quite early on, but still, the progression can be quite gradual at first.

I found with my mum that she flipped back and forth between some sense of 'reality' and complete confusion, which was one of the reasons it took me so long to get a diagnosis.

As the dementia progresses things become a lot more obvious and any general memory test (remembering 3 items, the year, the day, who the prime minister is) will quickly show the assessing doctor that there is something very wrong.

Your loved one may sometimes be referred for a brain scan to check for the plaques associated with dementia. Sometimes they will not do this. In the UK getting a diagnosis, and the right treatment, can still be a frustrating and prolonged process and having to fight and advocate for your loved one can become exhausting.

Falls and an unsteady gait can also be a sign, my mum had the distinct Alzheimer's shuffle and had several unexplained falls before her diagnosis.

Chapter 7

## Speak to Those Who Know

Sadly, even healthcare professionals don't always understand the complex needs of you and your loved one with dementia. When you watch first-hand someone's slow and heartbreaking descent into memory loss, confusion and delusion, you also become aware of their little quirks and behaviours.

When my mum was first put on Donepezil medication by a somewhat unhelpful and patronising doctor from the local memory clinic, I expressed concern about her taking medication in the right amounts and at the correct times. I was her only support then, and I was also looking after my young son and working part-time.

He flippantly suggested a days of the week pill box (a great idea for earlier stages but Mum was already far past this point by the time of her diagnosis). I looked at him incredulously and said, "But she doesn't know what day it is!" He put his hand up as if to shush me, as if I was just being difficult, and asked if it would be possible to come every evening before bed to give to her.

I stared in disbelief and said I could possibly do that for a few nights, but I don't drive, I have a young son and can't do it indefinitely. Again, he put his hand up to stop my questions, giving no further advice or support, and left me feeling contrite and somehow ashamed.

Although he was nothing but kind to my mother (even though she rolled her eyes at me throughout his questioning) I found him unhelpful and patronising towards me. Yet again I felt like I was alone with no support. I had already been advised she would not qualify for subsidised care (due to the savings threshold) and as she flatly refused to admit there was a problem (in her mind there wasn't) I just could not decide to put care in place for her myself. I needed advice, I needed a push in the right direction, and I needed to get over the patriarchal voice in my head that admonished

"This is your job, you're the daughter and you should be doing all of this."

I needed a tipping point, something out of my control, the Universe to tell me what to do. Anything. This was to happen about a year in the future, but more about that later.

You need to find a support group that gets what you're going through. If you have a friend or family member who has experience of dementia, reach out to them. I was lucky to have a local friend in an almost identical situation, also an only child. We compared stories, laughed and cried. She too feared her mum would never accept external care.

At the point where she could no longer cope, she was at a breaking point, a full-time carer was finally brought in by Adult Social Care. Even though this was by no means the end of her caregiving journey (this is a lifelong challenge for family members, even if care is in place) I saw the burden lift from her eyes, she looked brighter than I'd seen her in months, and it gave me hope for the future.

Though she still faces tough situations with her mum and care is not the fix-all solution for family caregivers, it is a necessary and wonderful support and if your loved one falls below the savings threshold, they may too qualify for help so please find out about it, even if you feel disloyal, even if you feel you can do it all, because at some point in future you may not be able to.

My friend was also a wonderful resource; she told me about many benefits that my mum could qualify for, despite her savings. Dementia sufferers can usually qualify for a Council Tax Exemption and depending on their needs, Attendance Allowance.

Mum also now has a door alarm, tracker and call service which links directly to a call centre. I didn't know about any of these free services because initially I was told if she had savings, she wasn't entitled to anything, this simply isn't true, and you must claim what you can as their savings will soon be poured into care. Every little you can get, take it.

You may also be entitled to some support; if you provide at least 35 hours of care to someone per week (this includes taking them to appointments, running errands, shopping for them) and they receive certain benefits (for instance Personal Independence Payment or Disability Living Allowance) you may be entitled to Carers Allowance.

In 2024 eligible carers were able to claim £81.90 per week, which isn't a lot I know, but a little extra which may help you, especially if you've had to quit your job or reduce hours due to your caring responsibilities. You can find out more at https://www.gov.uk/carers-allowance or speak to your local council.

## Chapter 8

### Tipping Point 1

Like many people with the early stages of dementia, my mum was in complete denial, she didn't think there was anything wrong. I tried in several calm (and not so calm if I'm honest) conversations to ask her to come to the GP with me, that I thought she was having memory issues, and begged her to believe me. I tried and tried to help her understand that there was something seriously wrong.

These discussions never went well; she would become angry, scream, cry … tell me it was me that had the problem, that I was trying to tell her she was mad. This went on for years and it was getting harder and harder to handle it on my own.

She'd call me at 6 am shouting at me because I'd said I was coming to see her that morning, I'd say I hadn't and that I was coming later. She would scream at me; and say I was the one with the memory problems. Accuse me of anything and everything.

Some days I'd go round, and she'd have lost all her painkillers and tell me someone must have broken in and taken them. I'd look around the house, worried that she may have taken too many, only to find all of them stuffed in a shoe or thrown in the bin. Misplacing and hiding objects is of course another common dementia sign, especially in the early and mid-stages.

About 6 months after my dad had died, I was walking my son to school with a friend and her son. When we were halfway there my mobile started ringing, and I could see it was Mum calling. My heart sank as it always did now, the sound of the ringtone causing my stomach to clench and my head to start pounding.

I answered, "Hi Mum everything ok?"

She sounded upset "I don't know where Dad's gone. I haven't seen him all morning. Have you seen him? I'm getting worried."

Ice poured through my veins; it was getting worse. I asked my friend to take my son to school and I tried to explain to Mum that Dad had passed away months ago. She was shocked momentarily but then seemed to accept it. Said of course she knew this.

This was the start of many upsetting and worrying phone calls and she would flip back and forth between knowing he was dead and thinking she'd seen him. I was still grieving myself and dealing with this was devastating. I didn't know what to do or where to turn. I kept trying to persuade her to see the GP with me, but it was useless.

There comes a point when most experts advise to go along with their delusions. Unfortunately, there is a midway point (or at least there was for my mum) when if I didn't tell her what had happened, she would keep calling me and worrying about where he'd gone. Nowadays I go along with whatever she says, however strange and if she asks where dad is, again rare these days, I say he's probably at work and will be back later. It's a tough road to navigate but you will become an unwitting expert at predicting their moods and needs.

One day when I was out with my boy and another friend and her son in London (we had been on a tour of Buckingham Palace) I received a frantic call. Mum said she had been calling all day – this was not true – I had no missed calls on my phone so whoever she was calling, it wasn't me.

She had hurt her ankle badly, it was swollen and bruised but she was managing to walk a little and refused to go to the doctor or hospital. I stayed with her until bedtime that night, helped her get upstairs and into bed and told her to wait for me in the morning so I could help her get up and see if I could persuade her to get checked out.

When I arrived in the morning she was already up and downstairs, but in a terrible mood. She accused me of stopping her from going to the hospital and said she'd hurt her ankle weeks ago, when it had only been the day before.

I managed to persuade her to go to the hospital and get an X-ray and to cut a long story short, this led to the diagnosis of a fracture and then the discovery that she has osteoporosis. We attended the Dexa scan together and two weeks later I sat with her at the GP while they explained her options to her. She took it remarkably well, I had dreaded it, and the GP prescribed Aledronic Acid which was the first course of treatment in osteoporosis. She would need to take it first thing in the morning, on an empty stomach, and sit upright for at least an hour to avoid nausea.

Mum had still not had her Alzheimer's diagnosis at this point, I just couldn't work out a way to get her to the GP to discuss her memory as she wouldn't agree there was any issue. However, during this discussion, I was desperate for help and willed the GP to see the stress I was carrying around with me.

I asked the GP what would happen if Mum forgot to take it at the right time, or accidentally took too many. I was desperate for her to see that there was another and more urgent issue here, that I dare not mention for fear of backlash and hours of retribution afterwards.

The GP looked me straight in the eye and said, "Do you have concerns about your mother's memory". I longed to say yes!! To say there was something very wrong and that I thought she had dementia, and that it was probably the stress of it all that had caused my dad's death, and I couldn't take it anymore. I was drowning, and I didn't know how I would get through each day because it was so hard to deal with her outbursts, repeated conversations and aggression.

But instead, I laughed it off and said, "No but we all forget things sometimes don't we, especially when we're getting older". I just couldn't say it in front of my mum, fear and misplaced loyalty prevented me. I had missed my chance. The light switched off again.

As it happened Mum decided not to take the medication as she read and re-read the side effects and flatly refused. I managed to get her to agree to take Evacal (high-strength calcium and vitamin D) for her bones and I hoped that would help.

I printed out the literature about osteoporosis that the GP had sent to me and left it with Mum. She said she wasn't surprised she had it and was so upbeat about it all, I was frankly amazed. I wrote a letter on behalf of her saying that she would take the Evacal but didn't want to take anything else, I got her to sign it because I knew if we went to the GP again, she would say she didn't know anything about any of it.

Six months later Mum and I were chatting one day, and she said something that made me realise she had forgotten about the diagnosis and didn't know what the Evacal tablets were for. I said they were for her osteoporosis. She said she didn't have osteoporosis; I reminded her that we'd spoken to the GP six months earlier.

She got upset, screamed at me, and said I'd never told her that she had osteoporosis, that she may as well be dead. She reacted now how

I'd expected her to react at the beginning. She told me I'd lied to her; I tried to prove to her I hadn't. I told her I'd taken her to the bone density scan that had led to the diagnosis.

Somehow it was all my fault; "Whatever you say!" she spat, "You are *always* right, aren't you!" These constant interactions were destroying my mental health, I was suffering from low-level depression and chronic anxiety, and yet I still somehow felt it was a betrayal to talk about her memory issues, without her consent. I should have done it earlier and I urge any of you out there reading this, not to leave it so long – speak to your GP, behind their back, if necessary, they need help and so do you.

There comes a time when their wishes are not as important as their needs. There comes a time when they don't know what's best for them and as they usually don't know that they have dementia, you will have to take control, as hard as this is.

They'll fight you; they'll hate you at times, and you will hate yourself. But you know deep down that they need professional help and so do you.

I was on the brink of getting help for her, making the move and reaching out. I kept putting it off, I was becoming scared of her and her outbursts and didn't want to rock the boat.

But I knew things couldn't go on the way they had been. The house was getting dirty and if I offered to help Mum would take it as an insult.

Since her fractured foot, I'd bought her foods that were easy to eat (ready-made sandwiches, salads etc) and she'd stopped even heating up soup.

Her care needs were increasing and her hallucinations and confusion about my dad were becoming much more frequent and disturbing.

Chapter 9

**Dealing with Delusions**

I found the early stages of Mum's dementia very hard, mainly because a lot of her anger and frustration was aimed at me.

Everything that has been written about dealing with dementia sufferers' false memories and delusions says to go along with them, humour them and don't disagree.

This really is the best advice, but I found it a struggle and couldn't quite bring myself to apologise for things I hadn't done. Looking back this was a mistake. They don't know what they're saying and what they think may be false, but it's true for them.

One day my partner and I arrived at Mum's house to take her to the dentist, she'd not been for many years and had got an abscess which had caused her face to swell. I'd signed her up with my dentist and made an appointment to take her.

When I arrived, she was angry and glaring at me. I asked if she was ready to go for her appointment. She said to me "Who IS Charlie anyway?" My heart sank.

By this point I'd been with my partner for over 9 years, we lived together, bought a house together, had a child together, and my parents saw him all the time.

I said to her that I'd been with Charlie for years, that she'd known him for years. That he was Jamie's father and that she came to our house regularly.

She raged at me "I never knew that! Did Dad know? You never told me that Jamie was my grandson. I didn't know he was his father."

Occurrences like this were becoming more and more frequent and it was making me stressed and anxious, I never knew what mood she would be in or what she would have imagined I'd done wrong.

I managed to appease her and get her to the dentist's surgery. I checked in with the receptionist and we sat down, but the accusations continued.

The conversation carried on and I tried to tell her we'd talk about it later; she shouted at me "I don't care WHO you sleep with just don't lie to me about it".

I was mortified and the receptionists pretended not to listen but were amused by the conversation.

This became a weekly occurrence. Mum not knowing who my partner was, shouting that she'd not know she had a grandson. I would show her pictures of us all together at our favourite local pub, pictures of her at the hospital the day my son was born; she would still say that she didn't know, and I'd never told her.

This stage was also the point that Mum started to talk to photographs and the TV. This is a common symptom among dementia sufferers but can be quite alarming for those around them.

The first time I arrived at Mum's house, and it happened, I didn't know what to think. She'd placed my graduation photo and a photo of my late sister on the table in front of her, facing the TV.

When she first answered the door (this was when she was still mobile) she said, "I've been chatting to the girls".

I was confused until I took my coat off and went into the living room, seeing the photos.

"We've been having a nice chat."

I still thought maybe she was kidding around or maybe she'd been feeling lonely, I know that when her parents passed, she still liked to talk to photos of them as if they were there.

I went out to make tea, my heart racing. I came back in with tea and some biscuits.

She said, "Can I give one to the girls?"

My heart sank. I gave her two biscuits and she placed one next to each frame.

This was the start of months of this type of behaviour. One day my son and I arrived to find that she'd lined up all his school photos, of varying ages, on the table in front of her.

She happily said, "I've got the boys here", and told me which one was shy, and which one was the cheeky one. My son tried to explain to her that they were all photos of him, but it fell on deaf ears, and I told him to let it slide.

I found this period difficult to deal with; sometimes I'd arrive, and she would have taken the photos out of their frames, or she'd tried to feed them and there would be yoghurt or chocolate mousse smeared over glass.

Once I got my head around it, I decided that it was harmless enough and if it brought her some joy, bringing out her mothering instincts, then it was fine.

However, things started to escalate and sometimes she'd call me several times in an evening to say that "No one had come to pick the boys up" and she was worried as she couldn't look after them forever.

I didn't know what to say. I'd try to tell her they were just photos; she didn't understand. I'd say not to worry and that their parents would come and get them later, to just keep them with her for the night.

This was before she had carers when she was still able to use the telephone, and these conversations could go on for hours without a break.

Sometimes I would remove the photos for a few days, then put them back. I didn't know if the joy they gave her was enough to counteract the worry of thinking she had multiple children to look after, feed and keep safe.

She doesn't talk to photos anymore. That phase has gone, and sometimes I miss it. I miss seeing her in mothering mode, I miss hearing her talk to 'them', and I miss her being more verbal and animated.

And that's the funny thing about dementia,
you'll miss a lot of things that break your heart
at first.

But during this time, I knew things were getting
worse, and that I had to get help. I was ready to
contact the GP, I couldn't take it anymore …
then came the pandemic.

Chapter 10

**Covid 19**

Suddenly the papers were full of stories about a flu-like illness in China, something that could potentially be life threatening. I remember talking to a mother acquaintance at the school gates, she was saying that we wouldn't be able to visit family, and that we'd have to stay indoors.

I was worried; Mum relied on me to get her shopping, sort out her bills, take her to the hairdressers each week, and more importantly for company and to keep her grounded in some kind of reality.

When the lockdown happened, I was at a loss to know what to do. I knew I wasn't supposed to see her; she had no official diagnosis at this point, and I would be essentially breaking the law by visiting her.

For six distressing weeks I'd tried to stay away; my partner would drop shopping to her every other day, I would write her a note and try to talk to her on the phone. She didn't understand what was going on and I was finding the whole situation traumatic.

She would tell me that someone had come into her house and was speaking to her in 'sign language', I can only assume this was the person who signed during the Covid press briefings from Number 10.

She also started calling me two, three, four times a day to ask where my dad was. We would talk around in circles, she would get upset, and I would have to pretend that the phone had cut out. It was impossible.

Then in week 5 or 6, her heating stopped working. The boiler had packed up and I needed to get someone around to fix it. This was ridiculous, I had to see her. I felt like a criminal going round to her house – the streets were largely empty; some people were wearing masks.

I arrived, expecting Mum to be over the moon to see me. I don't think she even realised I'd been missing from her life for 6 weeks. I tried to keep a mask on, but she couldn't hear me.

A friend of mine whose mum also has Alzheimer's said her GP had said to class her mother as vulnerable and therefore part of her social 'bubble'. So, this is what I did too, she had no support aside from me, and the six weeks of solitude had already caused a massive deterioration in her cognitive functioning.

By the time the lockdowns were over she had lost the small amount of routine she had had, and things never really got back to how they'd been.

Add to this the stress of home-schooling my son, navigating this unprecedented time of global chaos, and being isolated from friends, my mental health continued to take a massive battering, and I felt like I was losing my grip on reality. Looking back, I should have reached out to the GP sooner, but hindsight is 20/20. I would have done a lot of things differently but can't go back in time. But if you're at the beginning of this journey with a loved one, I hope my story

can help you. Please reach out, get help,
and contact dementia support groups. You're
not alone, you're not alone, you're not alone.

Chapter 11

**Tipping Point 2**

Not long after the world opened up again, Mum had another fall, this time while I was there.

I heard a crash at the bottom of the stairs and rushed to assist her. She was shocked but seemed ok, I managed to get her up and although her knees became badly bruised after an hour, she didn't seem to have injured herself too badly.

I stayed for most of the day and later that day she said her knees were hurting. I said she'd fallen down the stairs earlier, she looked at me blankly and said she hadn't.

Her short-term memory was getting worse, and I couldn't cope anymore. She fell asleep in her armchair and I fired off a desperate email to her GP confessing that I thought she had a memory issue, about her falls, and her hallucinations and delusions.

I read it through and pressed send, no turning back. I had delayed for too long out of fear and some misplaced sense of loyalty. She would kill me for doing this. But she didn't know anything was wrong.

No turning back. I arranged a private telephone conversation with her GP. It was emotional and she was kind.

I explained that Mum was in complete denial that there was anything wrong, so we managed to get her to the surgery under the guise of a health check.

Even so, when I arrived at her house to pick her up that day Mum had forgotten about the 'health check' and it was touch and go whether I'd be able to get her out of the house.

She glared at me the whole time and I was struggling to get her to keep her mask on (this was still a requirement in healthcare settings at that time).

Mum is also quite deaf (she never got to grips with the hearing aids we got for her shortly after Dad's death) so when people were wearing masks it was pretty much impossible for her to understand what was going on.

We sat in the surgery, Mum looking daggers at me and declaring quite loudly that it was a dump. Although it was her surgery from childhood, she no longer recognised it.

Mum was in a terrible mood and for once I was happy about it; I needed the GP to see her at her worst to get a referral to the memory clinic.

Eventually, her name was called, and we went into the consultation room. Mum was suspicious and defensive. I spoke to the GP and said, "Mum is a little upset with me as I forgot to tell her about the appointment." it's always better to blame yourself, as hard as this is.

The GP was kind, took her blood pressure and weighed her.

Then she did a quick and subtle assessment of her memory. She asked my mum her full name, this was ok. She asked her to give her home address, Mum looked at me, she couldn't remember it, although this was the house she'd lived in for over 50 years, the house I'd grown up in.

The GP asked some other questions; did she have any grandchildren, how many? She looked at me "How many do I have". My heart sank but this was just what the doctor needed to see "Just one Mum, my son Jamie."

We wrapped up the appointment and the GP said she would call me later. She arranged for a referral to the memory clinic, which I mentioned at the beginning of this book, however, this was just the start of a very difficult process to get extra support and care for her.

However, the wheels were turning. The fact that I'd told someone else about her memory issues felt like a massive betrayal, but also an immense relief.

## Chapter 12

### Tipping Point 3

Post covid life was beginning to get back to 'normal' I had my son's friends around; they were being boisterous as boys can be, and I was in the kitchen rustling up some chicken nuggets and chips.

Suddenly my phone rang, and it was my mum. She said there was a man in the house, she was upset and distressed. My first thought was that she was hallucinating; by this point, she would often say she'd seen my (dead) father, friends had been around when they hadn't, and she talked to the TV and photographs.

My partner raced round and called me to say that, sure enough, her back door had been broken into. Luckily the intruder had done a runner, and nothing had been taken.

I called the police and got a cab around with my son and myself. When the police arrived, I had to speak to them in advance of them interviewing Mum.

She had already told me three slightly different versions of events and so I told them that she had undiagnosed memory issues.

The police officer asked if she was under social care, and I said that I was waiting for a memory clinic assessment and social care visit. They said they would put a referral in so that hopefully I would get seen quicker.

They recommended getting a video doorbell or some kind of monitor and they were fantastic. I felt seen, they were kind to me and her, and it was a relief.

This nudged things in the right directly and soon she got the memory assessment that led to her being diagnosed and prescribed medication.

## Chapter 13

### Hide and Seek

As I mentioned earlier, hiding things is a common dementia trait and one that can be of great distress to both the person who can't find something and their frazzled caregivers.

My mum would regularly tell me that someone must have broken into her house and stolen her glasses/pain killers/lipstick and was not convinced when I'd say that no one would go to all the trouble of breaking in just to swipe her half-used make-up or prescriptions specs!

They will always look for a reason why they can't find something and as they can't remember squirrelling it away, they look for the next most logical (to them) answer.

The remote control for the TV was frequently put in her handbag, bedside drawers or elsewhere. I would have to hunt the house to find it and when I wasn't there, she would give up and pull the TV plug out from the socket. The following day I would get a phone call saying the

TV was broken. I'd go around and plug the TV back in. This would happen all the time. Top tip: you can get covers to prevent them from doing this! I wish I'd known this sooner.

Other times she'd lose her glasses which she needs to wear all the time. I'd find them in the laundry basket, under the covers of her bed, under the bed. I started to get to know her hiding places and find ways to keep stuff from going awol.

I got an identical remote control for her TV and would keep it stowed away in a drawer so that if she misplaced one, we would have another.

I did the same with her reading glasses. Hid the spare pair away so that if the worst should happen, she would still be able to see.

Hiding can be frustrating when it comes to trackers and SOS pendants. These can be very helpful when an elderly person is living on their own, but sadly when they have dementia they can lose or hide it, and you will have to be responsible for charging and keeping track of it.

In the early stage, however, technology can be useful; tracking devices, SOS alarms, watch GPS watches, CCTV-style cameras, and video doorbells can be a godsend; I will address this in later chapters.

They may also start throwing items away; one day before my mum had outside care, she called me in distress saying all her underwear had gone and she'd not been wearing any for 'months'. I knew this wasn't true, but I also believed her when she said she had none.

I went around and sure enough, her underwear drawer was empty. I'd found one pair of knickers thrown away in a plastic bag – I think this was when the incontinence was beginning.

Of course, I immediately popped to the shops and bought her several multipacks of underwear. She was very angry with me, however, as if it was all my fault. Anger towards a caregiver is usual; you are the person they will lash out at, it's not fair but it's just how it is.

Try not to take it personally, they know not what they do. It's hard, but keep reminding yourself it's the disease, it's not them.

Chapter 14

**Tipping Point 3**

Mum had been on the dementia medication for a few weeks, I was struggling to keep on top of her dosage and when I asked the GP for a repeat prescription, they said she wasn't due any, so I realised she'd been taking too many.

A few nights later I got a phone call from an unknown number at 5 am; never a good time for your phone to ring and never anything you want to hear.

It was a police station saying they'd found Mum wandering in the dark. I was devastated; I knew this was a risk with dementia but as she was frail and didn't tend to venture out on her own, I never thought it would happen. This was the first of many outings.

My partner, our son and I dressed at the speed of light and got ourselves in the car and over to Mum's house. When we arrived, she was sitting with a lovely WPC enjoying a cup of tea, there were also two male police officers.

Mum didn't know what all the fuss was about; a dog walker had alerted the police as they'd seen her shuffling down the road, it was dark as it was wintertime, and she seemed confused.

She'd told the police officers that she'd just come out of the cinema and was on her way home, "I told them I came from a good family, and I have a good Mum".

I chatted to the police officers privately and explained she'd just been diagnosed with Alzheimer's but wouldn't accept that she needed care and that I thought she'd been taking too many tablets.

They were very kind and suggested I speak to the GP again and get Mum some kind of tracking or monitoring device.

I stayed overnight and by the next day, Mum had no recollection of what had happened. I bought her a tracking device keyring which gave me some peace of mind, although one night the alarm went off and the tracker on my phone showed her location as somewhere at least a mile away from her house.

We threw ourselves in the car and went round to her house only to find her asleep in bed. Trackers can be a very helpful tool, however, especially if your loved one is still in the early stages and going out by themselves.

My next step was to get her a hallway video monitor. This was much more useful and alerted me to how much Mum was hallucinating during the day. There is a grey area of consent around this, but I spoke to Mum about installing it, using her prior falls as a reason and she agreed. As I am also her POA for health and financial affairs I know it is in her best interest to monitor her activity during the day to prevent her being a danger to herself or others. It also enabled her to stay in her own home independently for longer without supervision, so it's always worth considering. Please get consent from your loved one, ask for advice, and ensure a healthcare professional is aware of their lack of capacity.

I hoped it would also help alert me if she wandered again, but unfortunately, as she was constantly in the hallway rearranging ornaments and talking to herself, the next time she left and got picked up by the police, I missed her leaving.

It's important to say that by this point Mum had no sense of 'home' or where she was going. In other words, she was not able to go out alone and find her way back, so it was not safe for her to do so.

On this occasion, her neighbours had seen her chatting to police in a car and alerted me that she'd been picked up again.

After this, we installed a video doorbell which has been a godsend. This alerts me if she wanders and if we see her leaving, we jump in the car and go round. As her mobility is so bad, she rarely gets beyond the end of her path.

This has its drawbacks too; I am always 'on call' even when I don't go to see her. I can never really stop worrying about her. She does now have some care in place, which I will tell you about later, but between visits she has still been known to wander, even on weeks when she's barely been able to get out of her chair or stand up unaided.

Dementia can give them amazing physical strength and if she gets it into her head that she needs to go 'home' (her childhood home) then off she goes, usually always with her handbag, even if she's not properly dressed or shoeless, the handbag is still with her.

Just when I think this will be the last time she wanders, the alert will sound on my phone, and I'll see her shuffling out of the house.

Often, she'll try immediately to get back in, pressing on the doorbell. Most of the time I hear the alert, and we stop what we're doing and all pile in the car and drive around there.

I call her neighbours to ask them to intercept her. We get her back into the house; I make her a cup of tea and give her a custard cream and she's usually ok.

Occasionally she will be distressed and keep saying she needs to go home. Luckily now she has four care visits per day and an overnight care, so I can leave safe in the knowledge that she'll be checked in on regularly.

Chapter 15

**Homeward Bound**

Wanting to 'go home' is a common dementia sign. When my mum started talking about needing to go home, I would try and persuade her that she was already home, in the house she'd lived in for over 50 years.

Sometimes she'd believe me, sometimes not. I made her a memory book featuring pictures of the house with her, me as a child, and my father in. I had to find pictures of the house that still looked as it does today, I used one of those photo-gift websites to create a little picture book of our lives in that house, when they moved in, when I was born, and so forth.

It helped to some extent for a short while. But often I would arrive at her house to find she'd packed three carrier bags of possessions, and she'd be waiting for me to take her home.

Or I'd be out in London with my partner and our son, and she'd start calling me, asking me when she was going home.

I tried every tactic, but it didn't work. Sometimes I'd be at her house, and she'd say, "Well I'd better be going home now." I'd try and tell her this was her home, and she didn't need to go anywhere.

Sometimes she'd seem to understand, then I'd get up to leave and she'd say, "Well I'd better be going home too".

It was exhausting and went on and on and on. I was constantly worried about her leaving the house, constantly on high alert and something had to give.

Another issue was mail; every piece of post she received she would worry about. Most of the bills were paid by direct debit but she'd call me and say she'd had to pay a bill. I'd explain they got paid by direct debit, but she wouldn't know what this meant.

I'd try to explain it to her, but she'd then read the bill, THE WHOLE BILL, to me again, as well as the small print. Over and repeatedly. I'd often have to pretend to be cut off as the conversation could go on for an hour or more. They get stuck in a loop and sometimes you just need to break that loop.

There are some great insights on the Alzheimer's Society website about how to deal with someone who keeps asking to go home, I would urge you to read them.

Remember in their head their actual home, at this moment at least, is not familiar to them and no matter what you say, this is not what they are feeling or seeing.

## Chapter 16

### Forget Me Not

Now the hard part. Talking about your loved one forgetting who you are. While some dementia sufferers may always know their close family members, a large majority will not.

In the early stages of Mum's memory loss, I remember speaking to an elderly lady at the local church. I had taken my son to an Easter event there and a mutual friend had pointed me in her direction as she had experience with her own mother.

We chatted and I explained what had been happening since my dad's death. She was so kind and sympathetic, and said "Does she still recognise you?" I was taken aback, of course she did! I could never imagine her not knowing who I was.

I realised at that moment that we were still at the very early stages of the whole thing and hoped and prayed that this would never happen.

But it did. Before a stay in hospital that finally triggered additional care being put in place, I started to realise that she didn't always know who I was.

I can't remember the exact moment or conversation, but I can remember how I felt, devastated. We went through a phase of this when some days she seemed to know I was her daughter, others she wouldn't.

On some occasions when it happened and I said I was her daughter and she was delighted, would say "That's wonderful, I'm so glad!"

But on others, it did not go so well. One particular day, I told her I was her daughter, and she got terribly upset and confused. She said that no one had told her that I was her daughter and asked me "Did Dad know???" I said of course he knew, and he probably assumed she knew given the fact she'd given birth to me!

There's no logic to the things they think, and it doesn't matter what you say. On this occasion, Mum was in floods of tears as she thought I'd been taken away from her, that she hadn't raised me and that everyone had lied to her. I found it exhausting. I stopped trying to tell her who I was after that.

One other time, after she had carers, I got a frantic call from her main carer. Mum had been up all night looking for "Heidi" and was raging at the poor lady as she'd thought she'd left the door open, and I'd run away.

The carer asked me to go round and help calm her as Mum had gone out in the street to look for me, and the neighbours had been concerned with all the shouting.

When I got around, they were on the front doorstep. The carer said, "Look, Mrs Gloria, It's Heidi, your daughter!" Mum took one look at me and said, "You're not Heidi you're too big!"

I can laugh about it now, but at the time it was awful. Mum was upset, I was upset. She was looking for little 'me', the me that was in her reality that day. I wasn't who she wanted to see.

After these events, I used to go around not knowing what to expect. I would look for clues, if she referred to my dad as Pete, I would know that on that day, she thought I was a friend.

On other days she might say "Dad" and I knew I was her daughter again. These days don't happen anymore. I miss it. I miss her memories of my childhood, of family moments, that history of 'us' is now gone. Locked away somewhere in her mind.

In some ways, it's easier, as her daughter I got a lot of the blame for what was happening and things she couldn't control.

Now I'm just a friend, or maybe she thinks I'm one of the carers, though she never really understood she had carers. All I know is that on good days she likes me and tells me so. Or tells me she loves me. The love remains even though she's forgotten the reason for that bond.

## Chapter 17

**The Final Tipping Point**

Around the time of my 50<sup>th</sup> birthday, almost 5 years after Dad's passing, I arrived at Mum's one afternoon and couldn't find her. My first thought was that she'd wandered again, but eventually, I found her on the floor next to the bed.

She seemed ok but didn't know how she'd got there or what had happened. I asked if she could get up, but she said she couldn't.

I tried to help her but thought better of it as she has osteoporosis, I knew it was wise to call the paramedics in case she had a fracture or break.

I got her a pillow and a blanket (she was naked from the waist down but with her handbag – I later found a pair of wet knickers in the bag) and went to call an ambulance.

The ambulance guys were lovely; kind and empathetic, not just to her, but to me. They said that as she couldn't tell us what had happened or how she fell we would need to go to the hospital.

Looking back, I think they could see I was struggling too and were throwing me a lifeline. Mum spent two nights in a local hospital. She was scanned and examined and underwent various memory tests and blood tests. Aside from the obvious memory issues she hadn't broken anything, not a bruise on her.

I spoke at length to several healthcare professionals, all of whom had a slightly different opinion of what should happen with Mum's care going forward; but the consensus was that she needed care in place at home and that I needed some help.

This was what I needed. To be told what to do so that the decision was taken out of my hands. They put in 6 weeks of funded care (paid for by the council despite her savings) and this started us on the path to the next stage of the dementia journey.

Very quickly after returning from the hospital the council fitted a key safe, bathroom aids, door alarm and tracker/phone.

The whole event had been a blessing in disguise and what I needed to move forward. My misplaced loyalty to my mum's wishes had stopped me from getting the care she and I needed for too long.

Getting carers in for my mum was by no means the end of it, but it did mean I was supported, she was back in the system, and I had to change my attitude.

At this point, it's not always about what they want, but about what they need, and it took me a long time to realise this.

I've been lucky with Mum's carers, and she has two, maybe three lovely women taking care of her. At the beginning of her care journey, she needed support with washing and dressing.

The carers also gave her meals and supervised her medication, she had not been washing or eating properly. Now three years down the line, she's incontinent of both urine and faeces and we've moved her bedroom downstairs.

After another OT (occupational therapy) assessment recently she has a hospital bed, electric recliner chair, perching stool (for when she is washed) a commode on wheels. I purchased a walking frame which has helped the carers to get her up and moving.

Sometimes she refuses to be washed, and I often used to arrive to find her naked from the waist down after some accident. Her dignity is slowly being stripped away by this awful disease.

I try and find easier clothes for her to wear, trousers with elasticated waists, Velcro fastening skirts and the like.

She is unable to dress unaided any longer and sometimes even the carers and myself can't get her stand up to be cleaned, put on clean incontinence underwear and fresh clothes.

What these carers do is amazing, and they should be paid more and get the recognition they deserve. This goes too for family caregivers who whilst entitled to Carers Allowance need more financial support and assistance, especially if they have had to quit their job to assist their loved one.

My friend whose mother also has dementia once said, "I don't want to be her carer anymore, I want to be her daughter again". A sentiment which hit me at my core.

I am lucky to have care in place, I know I could not do it without this support. I find the incontinence difficult; Mum's mood swings are sometimes heartbreaking and upsetting, and whilst I have had to assist her carer to clean and change her on occasion, I find this side of caregiving both mentally and physically challenging.

I worry about what will happen when her money runs out and hope the council will step in and pay for her care. Once savings drop below the threshold (currently £23,250) the council will means-test her, and potentially supplement her care.

If your loved one is going into a care home the cost of their home may also be considered, meaning their property will need to be sold to pay for care home fees.

Currently, this does not apply if they are to stay in their own home with care in place. At this point, it may be up to you to prove that their needs can be met at home and that it is in their best interests to stay there.

## Chapter 18

### Sharing the Care

When carers first came in, I was relieved but initially, even more stressed out. Like any parent who's left their child at nursery for the first time, you fret about your ageing loved one, especially those with dementia.

I made sure I met her carers, there were a few on a rota at the start, and introduced myself and explained Mum's likes, dislikes, quirks and interests. I typed up a little note and put it in the blue book from the agency, so if any new carers come, they would be able to read it.

The thought that strangers would be letting themselves into Mum's house each day via the key safe made me feel wretched and guilty.

However, after the first few days of care, Mum started to look fresher, cleaner and better than she'd looked in ages.

I'd asked her if she'd seen anyone that morning and she'd say no. She didn't even know a carer had been, that she had carers, or that anyone was coming into the house.

She wasn't bothered when random people appeared in her living room, made her food, and helped her wash. That's how bad her short-term memory had become. I knew this was the right thing to do, she needed more than I could give her now and I needed the support.

It's now been almost three years since care has been in place. Mum's mobility has declined massively. Even with carers there is tremendous strain on myself and my partner and one of us is called there almost weekly to help the carer get Mum to stand up; she often slides off the chair onto the floor and then cannot or will not move.

As it's not a fall and we know she hasn't hurt herself my partner helps to lift her with the aid of a strap support. She often screams at the top of her lungs. It's horrible. Then five minutes she's ok again.

Overnight care has also now been put in place; as with many dementia sufferers, she is often awake during the night, sometimes mobile with her walking frame and the aid of her carer.

She then sleeps during the day. It's an impossible cycle to break, we've tried a few sleeping tablets, but they just made her more confused and didn't seem to help much.

I am in constant contact with the carers and still do her shopping, take her to healthcare appointments, do her tax return and sort out all medications and incontinence products; though in the last six months, I've had to push for a 'housebound' status for her, as getting her to appointments has become nigh on impossible. I worry about what will happen next, and what the next stage will be, but the only advice I can give is just take one day at a time. And try and switch off sometimes, take a moment for yourself if you can.

The trouble is with a dementia diagnosis we know there is no happy ending; however, they will have good days and so will you. Stop swimming against the tide, let the current take you and meet your loved one where they're at.

Her care is currently not full time and as she's self-funding money is dwindling quickly. During the time between carer visits, I listen out for the alert of the doorbell video from the app on my phone, in case she wanders, though it's becoming less frequent.

During those awful moments I realise she's left the house – last time wearing no shoes – I call the household together and we all bundle around and drive over to her house, which is thankfully not too far away.

She never gets far, her mobility is so bad, but it's stressful and traumatic. Sometimes I'll call her neighbours and ask them to meet her and make sure she doesn't get into any harm before we arrive.

When we get there, she just looks a little confused. We take her back inside, make her a cup of tea and it's as if it's never happened.

Going out for the day or even on holiday must be planned weeks or even months ahead. I must make sure she has full-time care during these periods because if she leaves the house and there's no one there to get her home, I don't know what will happen.

But I'm grateful that care is in place; before she had to accept help my partner, our son and I barely went away. If we did it would be a 48-hour break to the nearest coast and a night in a cheap hotel.

I couldn't leave Mum for that long, she would get confused, and I would have to ring her frequently – then if I couldn't get hold of her, I would panic.

I think back to those times, and I wonder how I coped and know that even though things are still hard, they're so much better than they were.

### I Miss You

I miss you Mum, yet you're still here,
You're someone else, I sometimes fear,
The things you say so strange at times,
I feel I'm going to lose my mind.

Sometimes I know you love me still,
But other times you rage until …
I have to go … walk from the room,
And calm myself, while darkness looms.

Day by day your memories fly,
It doesn't matter what I try,
You leave me more, each single day,
Sometimes I want to run away.

I tell myself "Remember, please …
It is not her but this disease".
But glares and stares cut to the quick,
It's not your fault, I know you're sick.

I'll fight to keep you safe from harm,
But there's no cure or lucky charm,
I have to watch you slip away,
It's just not fair, it's not ok.

I try to think of happy times,
Before Dementia stole your mind,
Your kindness, beauty, sense of fun,
But this disease we can't outrun.

Chapter 19

## Helping Children Understand Dementia

One of my biggest regrets about the past six years is that my son has seen a side to my Mum, his dear Nanny, that she would never have wanted him to see.

In the early stages, he was unaware, he was just 4 when my father died and her memory issues were at the early stages, I managed to keep the illness hidden from him and she was able to control her actions when he was around to some extent.

However, during the covid lockdowns, he started to see her strange behaviours and he was getting older. I was honest with him about her Alzheimer's and tried to explain to him that she didn't mean the things she said sometimes that it was the disease.

It was hard for him to understand, and I am currently working on a children's picture book to help other children in the same position.

Often her behaviours have made him cry; about a year ago we went around, and Mum accused me of keeping her locked in the house.

When I went to make a cup of tea, I heard her questioning him "Does she keep you locked up too? Does she let you go out".

My heart sank. I said to her she could go out whenever she chose and why didn't we get a taxi to the nearest coffee shop and go and have some cake.

She said nastily "Why do we need to get a taxi? I can walk there."

Her mobility issues mean that even walking to the end of her road is tricky, so I took a change of tack and said that it was quite a long walk, and Jamie didn't like walking that far.

She looked at me and accused me of not letting my son walk and screamed at the top of her lungs "YOU'RE EVIL!!!" at which point tears instantly streamed from my son's eyes.

I knew the carer was going to arrive in a short while, so I got up, got our stuff together, kissed Mum goodbye and said we'd see her tomorrow.

Sometimes it's better to leave the situation if you're able. The next day she'd forgotten the incident and that's another important thing to remember.

As the disease takes hold, their short-term memory is non-existent. Mum always forgets the arguments we have, sometimes less than half an hour later.

It's not their fault, keep this in your head. They would be devastated if they knew they'd said these things to you – don't let dementia win, keep them in your hearts.

Chapter 20

**The Fear**

If you're the blood relative of a loved one with dementia, you may also have 'the fear'. As well as worrying about their decline, you may also start to catastrophise your future and worry that you too will get dementia.

However, it's important to recognise that most dementias are not inherited; although in some rare kinds of dementia, there may be a genetic link, this only represents a very small percentage of overall cases.

There are also things you can do to help prevent cognitive decline in the future. Eat a healthy diet, limit processed foods, avoid stress and try to keep your brain active.

Learn new things, be social and try to keep a growth mindset. Paint, draw, learn a language and resist the urge to find solace in sugar and alcohol.

I always find comfort in the 'Nun Study' which was started by epidemiologist David Snowdon in 1986. In a nutshell, he tracked the health (both cognitive and physical) of 678 nuns at convents across the US. Findings showed that those who continued to learn and cultivated a positive mental attitude were less likely to display signs of dementia, even those who had a genetic disposition or were starting to develop the sticky amyloid plaques associated with certain dementias, continued to lead a healthy and cognitively sharp life.

The nuns who had an education of bachelor's degree or higher were also less likely to develop Alzheimer's in later life and often lived longer too.

There is evidence to prove that constantly learning new things can develop new neural pathways, thus giving your brain more chances to retain cognition, even if signs of deterioration are starting to show.

Vascular health was also an important factor in the Nun Study; after examining the brains of

102 nuns after their death, of the 61 who had the sticky plaques and tangled proteins which are associated with Alzheimer's disease, those who had not had or showed signs of having had a stroke, had not shown signs of dementia.

I urge you to check out the Nun Study, there are lots of great articles about it and pictures of some of the nuns who took part.

To simplify these are the things to keep in mind if you want to live a long and cognitively healthy life:

1. Look after your heart.
2. Keep active!
3. Check your hearing.
4. Eat healthily.
5. Stay socially connected.
6. Avoid knocks to the head.
7. Do activities you enjoy.

I would also add to this, to try and practice meditation and mindfulness. Avoiding stress is so important, and yet we as dementia caregivers may at times find this impossible.

However, talking to a therapist, practising meditation and trying to develop a positive mindset can help, not only with your ability to give care but will help to keep your body and mind healthy now and in the future.

Keeping a gratitude diary can help you focus on the positive things in your life, even if you feel there's nothing much to feel positive about right now. Write down anything you can think of each day to be grateful for, even if it's just a good cup of coffee, someone complimenting you, or having a roof over your head!

I also think it's important to remember that your loved one would not want you to be unhappy, they would hate what this disease is doing to them and you, so give yourself a break, you're doing the best you can. You are not alone.

## Chapter 21

### Enjoy the Good Days

I don't want you to think that there are no good days with dementia. In the early days, we managed to take Mum out to restaurants, shopping and to our house for Sunday lunches and special occasions.

Even now when her mobility is limited there will be times when she is happy to see me and we will laugh about things, even if sometimes the conversation is impossible to follow.

She loves biscuits, she always had a sweet tooth and takes obvious joy in eating them. Some days she is so happy to see me and tells me she loves me and I'm a 'Good Girl' or a 'Lovely person'.

She may not understand that I'm her daughter anymore, but she still loves and likes me (most of the time) and there is still a connection there.

I know the next stage may not be like this. I guess what I'm saying it hold on to the good times. We know that this journey will come to an end at some point and when it does you will miss them, even the hard moments you will miss.

Find things to do with them; if it's not too triggering show them old photos. If they used to like drawing or painting, try to do this with them. There are dementia-friendly books with large words and pictures, maybe about the region they grew up in, or celebrities or events from their youth.

You can also find lots of activity 'toys' online that will keep their hands busy, and their minds occupied, you can even get soft toys and 'pets' that give them something to care for and hold.

If their mobility is good, you could find out about day centres in your area; many councils run activity centres for the elderly, including dementia sufferers, where they can do craft activities, drink tea and talk with others. If you care for your loved one full time this could also give you much-needed respite.

Use the internet to find out about support, cafes and groups for you and your loved one. Try to take each day at a time and if your loved one has had a bad day, screamed at you, or shown aggressive or difficult behaviours say to yourself "Has anything actually happened?". What I mean by this is, that whilst dementia behaviours are incredibly upsetting, they are just that. If your loved one is safe, not in any danger, and has eaten and drank today then that's ok.

And always remember to reach out, you are not alone and you're doing an amazing job.

### Imperfect Life

Learn to love your imperfect life,
Its highs and lows, Its troubles and strife.
Each day is a blank slate, find glimmers of hope,
Resist the urge to scroll and mope.

Someone's life may seem better, it's true,
But there's someone out there who would love to be you.
The challenges faced make you who you are,
And good days are coming, they're never too far.

Happiness is an illusion, peace is the goal,
Instant gratification will not mend your soul.
Don't look outside to improve mental health,
Just focus within and come home to yourself.

Chapter 22

**It Gets Tougher but So Do You!**

I want to tell you your loved one with dementia will get better, and that things will get easier. Sadly, they will get tougher, but you know what? So will you … and what you would have thought impossible to deal with a few years ago you will do as if it's second nature.

As I write this, I am at my mum's house after a worried call from her main carer. She's tearful and wet, I've managed to remove her adult nappy and have tried in vain to help to sit on the edge of the bed to stand.

I've tried to move her legs, but she screams in pain. She often screams at the slightest touch, also with anything hot or cold. The carer sometimes finds it hard to get her to accept personal care (washing) and adult wet wipes are often all that can be used.

I'm waiting for the carer to return for her lunchtime visit. I should be working; I get more and more behind on work every week.

Last night my partner had to come and help get Mum back into bed as she'd slipped off and onto the floor. It's becoming a regular occurrence and unsustainable I know, but the thought of having to make the care home decision is more than I can handle right now.

There will come another tipping point soon and my journey continues. Hold on, whatever happens, it will be ok. This journey is hard, but there will be moments of joy, and you will miss them when they go, though sometimes it feels like this would be a release for them and you.

Helping to care for someone with dementia will have its highs and lows, it will forever change you, humble you and make you a different person.

You are amazing, you're doing great, you're not alone. Please read this book and others like it to help you on your journey.

Look out for Instagram accounts which deal with dementia, there are some fantastic ones which will give you light-hearted yet practical advice about how to deal with certain situations and challenges.

Dementia is not fair, on them or you, but right now there is no cure or magic wand. Hopefully one day there will be, so give generously to charities which support research, and take part in sponsored walks, runs, and coffee mornings to help put a stop to this debilitating illness that has, for far too long, been written off as a natural part of ageing.

It's not a given that you will get dementia as you age, and we must continue to fight to find a cure.

## Custard Creams

You used to phone 10 times or more, but now you can't and phone no more.
I used to dread those frantic chats, but now I miss them, fancy that.
I'd watch the app in case you left, but now I get reprieve,
It seems you're bedbound, cannot walk, I'd give anything to see you leave.

The early stages you lashed out, we'd argue just like mum and daughter,
But now you barely understand, you smile but don't know who I am.
As time goes on you need me less, your care is now in place,
With gratitude, accept that help but feel I've been replaced.

You'll never greet me at the door, I'll never take you shopping,
Or share the memories of our past, this journey's one way, ain't no stopping.
Today I live for glimpses, signs of who you've been,
The joy upon your lovely face when eating custard creams.

## Chapter 23

### Update

This book has been a labour of love, started as notes on my phone, typed frantically during difficult days during the early stages of Mum's illness.

It's taken many years to complete and so with sadness, I need to write this update. The thing about dementia is that it affects the body too. Last April Mum stopped being able to walk entirely, even with a frame and support, and is now entirely bed/chair bound.

As a result of this, while waiting for a physiotherapist to train her carer and me on a patient transfer aid, Mum developed a DVT. This led to a stressful few days and an ambulance to A&E. After various tests and scans, it was discovered she had blood clots in her abdomen and lungs.

Outcomes for dementia patients in the hospital are not good, and I was there for most of her stay advocating for her.

The ambulance transfer was horrendous. She screamed, lashed out … hit me, and hit the paramedics, she was frightened and reactive, it was horrible to see.

The hospital stay was a mixed bag, and I was advised not to treat her blood clots (the quality-of-life debate always rearing its ugly head), although, after discussions with various doctors, I chose to treat her with Apixaban.

She was very unwell, but because of her poor physical health coupled with the dementia, she now needs two carers at a time, to move her with a hoist. By some miracle she qualified for Fast Track CHC funding which means, for now, her care is paid for, a tremendous relief, although still not full-time.

However, a month ago she became very unwell again and was admitted again to the hospital with severe and life-threatening anaemia, after a stressful week of trying to get blood tests done, chasing them up, and being fobbed off again and again.

After three transfusions and one iron infusion, she was discharged, but I have been told that she has unexplained bleeding in her body, which probably means cancer.

Because of her advanced Alzheimer's, further investigations were thought to be too traumatic. The transfusions themselves were awful for her; she lashed out, tried to rip the needle and tube out, and screamed in pain and fear.

I was with her for most of the time, being her voice, and trying to help keep her calm. I took two weeks off work, unpaid, and as her future prognosis is not good, I have reduced my work hours so that I can spend more time with her.

Her blood levels will be monitored but she is now under palliative care, her journey may soon come to an end, although my mum is a fighter, tough, and stubborn ... so only time will tell.

I have been asked to think about whether it's kind to put her through future transfusions. It's a decision I don't want to make and, as I type this, I'm still unsure of what I will do.

Some days she seems happy, laughs, and jokes around with me and the carers. On other days she's distraught, thinks her family and husband have abandoned her, and prays to God to fix her legs that will not walk and her brain that can't think.

She hates being changed, cleaned and moved and screams at the top of her lungs, hits, bites, and rages. Then afterwards says sorry. I don't know what quality of life she has, and whether the rare happy moments are enough.

The pressure on dementia family caregivers is immense, to make the right choice, to keep their needs and wants in mind, and to respect their wishes.

My friend M and I have started an Instagram account @dementiatalkwithM&H so that others can learn from our experiences. We want to raise awareness of this disease and the fact that family caregivers need more help, both financially and emotionally.

We now have over 1000 followers on Instagram and hope, when we have a little more time, to launch a podcast to help others in the same situation.

It's hard to look on the bright side when it comes to dementia, there aren't many positives. But we have found comfort in helping others, meeting other advocates at the Alzheimer's & Dementia Show earlier in the year, and connecting with other dementia care influencers.

Life can throw some difficult stuff your way sometimes, and you can choose to go one of two ways. You can feel resentful and crumble (that's what I was doing) or you can keep moving forward and try to make something positive come out of your dark times. I've done both and the latter is infinitely better.

I hope reading this has helped, I hope you feel seen, and please follow @dementiatalkwithM&H on Instagram if you'd like to join our community.

YOU ARE NOT ALONE.

Resources for dementia caregivers and those suffering from dementia:

**DEMENTIA ORGANISATIONS:**

**Dementia UK**

https://www.dementiauk.org/

Dementia UK is a specialist dementia nursing charity that is available to support not just the person with dementia, but the whole family. The website is informative, and you can also call them on 0800 888 6678 to speak to an Admiral Nurse.

**Alzheimer's Research UK**

https://www.alzheimers.org.uk/

Alzheimer's Research UK is full of useful information about the different types of dementia and how you can raise money for their charity. Many caregivers find this a positive thing to do for themselves and their loved ones.

**Alzheimer's Society**

https://www.alzheimers.org.uk/

Packed with practical information about dementia, daily living and legal/financial support the Alzheimer's Society is a tremendous resource. You can also call the Dementia Support Line on 0333 150 3456 and speak to trained staff who can give you the support you need. I found the Dementia Support Forum an immense comfort, you can post questions and let off steam – one of the moderators or others in your position help with advice or a friendly word.

**BOOKS & FILMS:**

Read books that will help you understand the disease; *Still Alice* by Lisa Genova (now a major film starring Julianne Moore) is one to consider. *The Father*, starring Antony Hopkins gives insight into how a dementia sufferer sees the world, there are lots of other practical books which will help you.

**Recommendations for adults:**

*The Alzheimer's Solution* by Dr Dean Sherzai & Dr Ayesha Sherzai (Publisher – Simon & Schuster UK)

*Somebody I Used to Know* by Wendy Mitchell (Publisher – Bloomsbury Publishing)

*The Dementia Caregivers Survival Guide* by Janet G. Cruz (Publisher - Unlimited Concepts)

Contented Dementia by Oliver James (Publisher -Vermillion)

**Recommendations for children:**

*My Grandma Has Dementia* by Alex Winstanley (Self-published and available on Amazon)

*Grandma, It's Me by YY Chan* (Publisher – Little White Flowers)

*The Tide by Clare Welsh* (Publisher – Little Tiger)

Milk Tulips

**SOCIAL MEDIA/INSTAGRAM RECOMMENDATIONS:**

@dementiadarling – Carrie Aalberts is a dementia caregiver educator and advocate. Her account is packed with helpful tips, inspirational posts, and more. She also has a podcast @gatherdarlings.

@dementia_careblazers – Dr Natali Edmonds is a dementia care expert and offers support for family members caring for a loved one with dementia. Follow her on Instagram and download her FREE Dementia Dose Newsletter.

@misspatticake – Follow Patti Lafleur's caregiving experiences; her Instagram account is full of stories and videos of her caring for her late mother. Inspirational and poignant.

@dementiasdaughter – This account talks about the challenges of Alzheimer's caregiving, sandwich caregiving and nursing home life. The account holder's mother has Alzheimer's, and her father had FTD.

@belightcare – Adria Thomson posts videos and daily posts for professional and personal caregivers. Another wonderful Instagram account to follow.

@dementiatalkwithM&H - Our account! Set up this year, myself and my friend Marielle. It's full of dementia caregiving tips, personal stories, and advice. We hope you follow along!

**TECH RECOMMENDATIONS:**

I'm not going to mention specific brands, but you can find these types of gadgets with any quick internet search, and they could be helpful, some you may also be able to get from your local council if your loved one has been diagnosed and meets certain criteria:

**Trackers** – you can get pendants, keyrings and even GPS insoles to help with wandering. If the person you're caring for is quite mobile and in the early stages these can be tremendously beneficial. Some also incorporate and SOS alarm which can link directly to a call centre or your phone if they are in trouble.

**Door alarms** – if there is no full-time care in place and you're worried about nighttime wandering there are door alarms which can link directly to an app on your phone or call centre.

**Video doorbells** – not only can video doorbells be helpful to keep track of wandering, but it also means you can see who's coming to the door. Dementia sufferers can be vulnerable for fraudsters so this way you can keep an eye on them and who is coming and going.

**Fall sensors** – sadly as dementia progresses, frailty can also become an issue with falls a common occurrence. If there is no care in place a fall sensor can be beneficial, they can be in pendant or 'watch' style form, though the only drawback is that dementia sufferers will tend to take them off, misplace or hide them if they're in the mid to late stages.

**Electric recliners** – if mobility and standing become problematic an electric recliner chair can be beneficial. One that enables the user to press a remote and get to a standing position can help them be independent for longer and can also help if they have a carer who must wash and clothe them. The council may be able to provide a chair if your loved one meets the criteria, if in doubt ask for an OT assessment.

**Universal remote controls** – if there's something that is frequently misplaced (in my mum's case the remote control) buy a replica or universal remote and keep it somewhere safe so you can use it if the other is lost.

**Mobility and care aids** – if your loved one also has mobility issues find out from your local council if they qualify for any free ones. Even though my mother has savings the council have provided an electric recliner, hospital bed, bath rails, bath seat, wheelchair and commode. Please find out what is available to you. You can also find these and other items such as walking frames online.

**Day of the week clocks** – these can be tremendously helpful in the early stages of dementia. You can go for a basic model which shows the time, date and day of the week and some also say whether it's morning or afternoon. Other hi-tech options can be programmed to remind your loved one to take their meds, eat lunch, drink water etc.